For my Great Niece Kaitlyn...
the sweetest girl I know
and love so very much...

Annie's Attitude on Bullying

Pamela Brown

Order this book online at www.trafford.com
or email orders@trafford.com

Most Trafford titles are also available at major online book retailers.

© Copyright 2010 Pamela Brown.

All rights reserved. No part of this publication may be reproduced, stored in a retrieval system, or transmitted, in any form or by any means, electronic, mechanical, photocopying, recording, or otherwise, without the written prior permission of the author.

Printed in the United States of America.

ISBN: 978-1-4269-6978-2

Library of Congress Control Number: 2011909980

Trafford rev. 08/12/2011

 www.trafford.com

North America & international
toll-free: 1 888 232 4444 (USA & Canada)
phone: 250 383 6864 ♦ fax: 812 355 4082

Annie's Attitude

on Bullying

My name is Tugboat Anabel, but everyone calls me Annie. I live with my mom and dad and my brothers Buddy, Scooter and Murphy. I also have a sister named Daisy. And then there is Lillie and Tank our two cats.

I am an English Bulldog. Sometimes my English Bulldog breed is called Bully for short...this is not to be confused with people Bullies...

I am sweet
and kind and I never push or shove or make anyone feel bad. I always try my best to make everyone around me feel happy.

People Bullies are not nice and you should never, never put up with being bullied.

If you are being bullied, you should always tell an adult.

Tell your parents, your teacher, your older brother or sister, any adult... but tell someone. It's when you stay silent that you give the Bully power to keep doing what he or she is doing.
Love, Annie

A Bully is...
Someone who pushes you around.
Never leaves you alone.
Tells you what to do.
Picks on you.
Calls you names.
Treats you badly.
Hurts you.
Takes your snack or lunch money.
Is mean to you.
Says hurtful things to you.
Shoves you.
Threatens you.
Beats you up.
Doesn't care about your feelings.
Embarrasses you in front of people.
Calls you nasty names.

Stick up for yourself!

Friends don't bully friends...

Remember:
Those who can, do...
Those who can't, bully...

Courage is fire
and
bullying is smoke...

Bullies thrive
wherever
authority is weak...

Don't be a prisoner
of being bullied...

Bullies will never
reach higher ground
if they are
pushing others down...

It's never okay
to make
fun of others...

Just say "NO"
to
bullying...

Bullies
are
Cowards...

If you're being bullied...
STOP
and tell someone...

You are not alone…
It's not your fault…
You can do something about it…

Communicate, tell someone
your parents, your teacher,
your brother, your sister,
your friends...

Stay away from bullies...
tell someone...
avoid bad situations...
make friends...
project confidence...
STAMP OUT BULLYING

www.ingramcontent.com/pod-product-compliance
Lightning Source LLC
Chambersburg PA
CBHW042019080426
42735CB00002B/109